Discovering My World

Animals in the Garden

by Melvin and Gilda Berger

SCHOLASTIC INC.

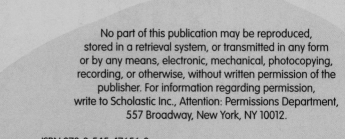

ISBN 978-0-545-47656-0

Copyright © 2013 by Melvin & Gilda Berger

All rights reserved. Published by Scholastic Inc.
SCHOLASTIC and associated logos are trademarks
and/or registered trademarks of Scholastic Inc.

12 11 10 9 8 7 6   16 17 18/0

Printed in the U.S.A.   40
First printing, March 2013

Photo Credits: Photo Research: Alan Gottlieb
Cover: © Brian Gadsby/Photo Researchers, Inc.; Back cover: © Stephen Dalton/Minden Pictures; Title page: © Shutterstock; page 3: © Shutterstock; page 4: © Shutterstock; page 5: © Linda Freshwaters Arndt/Photo Researchers, Inc.; page 6: © Juniors Bildarchiv GmbH/Alamy; page 7: © blickwinkel/Alamy; page 8: @ Aydın Mutlu/iStockphoto; page 9: © Rolf Nussbaumer Photography/Alamy; page 10: © Ocean/Corbis; page 11: © Juniors Bildarchiv GmbH/Alamy; page 12: © Shutterstock; page 13: © Shutterstock; page 14: © Duncan McEwan/Minden Pictures; page 15: © Philippe Clement/Nature Picture Library; page 16: © In Depth Imagery/Alamy

Who helps in the garden?

Birds help.

Which bird is eating an insect?

Birds eat insects that harm plants.

Spiders help.

Their webs catch insects that harm plants.

Ladybugs help.

Ladybugs eat bugs that harm flowers.

Toads help.

Toads eat snails.

Bees help spread pollen.

Butterflies do, too.

Does the worm's skin look smooth?

Worms make tunnels in the soil.

Loose soil helps plants grow.

Ask Yourself

1. Can you name two animals that eat bugs?
2. How do spiders catch bugs?
3. How do ladybugs help the garden?
4. Which animals spread pollen?
5. How do worms make the soil better?

You can find the answers in this book.